NOVEMBER

PATTERNS, PROJECTS & PLANS

by
Imogene Forte

Incentive Publications, Inc.
Nashville, Tennessee

Illustrated by Gayle Seaberg Harvey
Cover by Susan Eaddy
Edited by Sally Sharpe

ISBN 0-86530-127-1

Table of Contents

PREFACE

November – a bountiful month

NOVEMBER . . .

. . . A TIME of rich autumn colors – rust and red, orange and brown, black and gold, deep purple and burnt yellow.

. . . A TIME of harvest and plenty – ears of corn from golden fields, fruits and vegetables to fill cornucopias, sheaves of wheat to make muffins and breads.

. . . A TIME of busy activity – squirrels gather acorns and nuts; chipmunks and other animals prepare their winter homes; finely feathered fowl strut, squawk, and fly; birds fly south for the winter.

. . . A TIME of feasting and festivity – turkey and dressing, cranberries and fruit salad, sweet potatoes and wild rice, pumpkin pie and hot apple cider, family and friends of all ages.

All of this and more is the bounty of November waiting to be brought into your "come alive" classroom. Watch students' smiles widen and their eyes brighten as the bounty of November greets them from the ceiling to the floor, from windows and doors, from work sheets and activity projects, from stories and books, and especially from an enthusiastic, "project planned" teacher.

This little book of NOVEMBER PATTERNS, PROJECTS & PLANS has been put together with tender loving care to help you be prepared to meet every one of the school days in November with special treats, learning projects and fun surprises that will make your students eager to participate in every phase of the daily schedule and look forward to the next day. Best of all, the patterns, projects and plans are ready for quick and easy use and require no elaborate materials and very little advance preparation.

For your convenience, the materials in this book have been organized around three major unit themes. Each of the patterns, projects and plans can be used independently of the unit plan, however, to be just as effective in classrooms in which teachers choose not to use a unit approach. All are planned to complement and enrich adopted curriculum schemes and to meet young children's interests and learning needs.

Major unit themes include:
- Welcome, November!
- Turkeys And Other Fine Feathered Fowl
- Thanksgiving – A Time To Be Thankful

Each unit includes a major objective and things to do; poster/booklet cover, bulletin board or display; patterns; art and/or an assembly project; reproducible basic skills activities; and book, story and poem suggestions to make the literature connection.

Other topics, special days and events for which patterns, projects and plans have been provided include:
- National Children's Book Week (November 13-19)
- America
- It's Harvest Time For The Animals, Too
- Nutrition

Welcome, November!

Major Objective:
Children will develop awareness of the colors, sights, sounds, tastes, seasonal changes, and events that characterize the month of November.

Things To Do:

- Help the children use the patterns in this book to make decorations for doors, windows, desks, bulletin boards and bookcases.

- November is often called election month. Let the children color and cut out the patterns on page 22 Display the artwork on an "all American" bulletin board. (Add the Statue of Liberty, page 21, if desired.)

- Teach the children the pledge of allegiance if they do not already know it. Give each child a copy of the poster on page 20 to color and take home (or display the posters on the "all American" bulletin board).

- Observe National Children's Book Week (November 13-19)! Share beautiful picture books and "November" books (see pages 77 and 78). Give each child a library poster (page 19) and bookmarks (page 18) before taking the class to the library.

- Send the "letter to parents" (page 10) home to announce the month's activities and to ask for donations for your November materials collection. Check your supplies to be sure that you are ready for the month.

To complete the activities in this book, you will need:

- construction paper (assorted colors)
- **crayons & markers**
- rubber bands or string
- tape (cellophane & masking)
- paste
- scissors
- pencils
- stapler
- butcher paper (desired colors)
- newspaper
- small, medium & large brown paper bags

- hole punch
- yarn
- straight pins
- pipe cleaners
- toothpicks
- pine cones
- potatoes
- sticks (each approximately 15 inches)

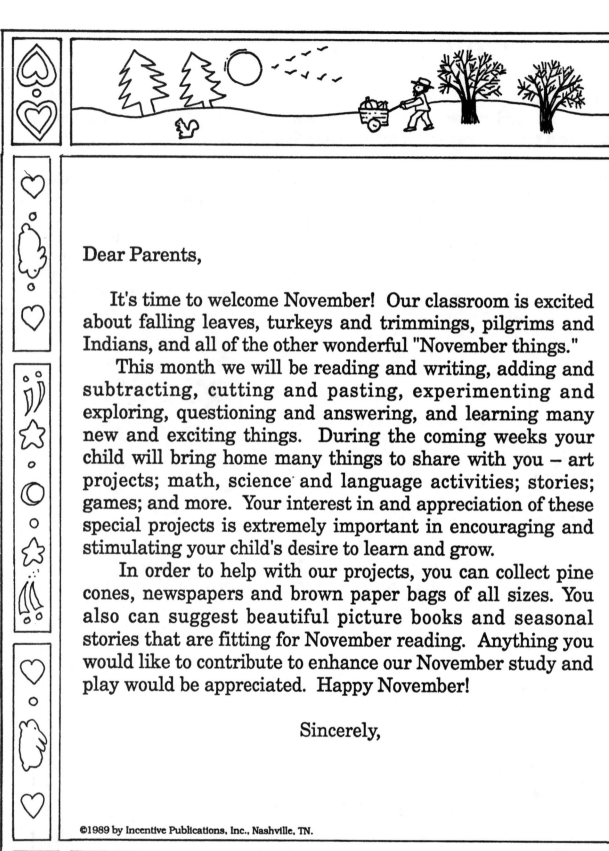

Dear Parents,

It's time to welcome November! Our classroom is excited about falling leaves, turkeys and trimmings, pilgrims and Indians, and all of the other wonderful "November things."

This month we will be reading and writing, adding and subtracting, cutting and pasting, experimenting and exploring, questioning and answering, and learning many new and exciting things. During the coming weeks your child will bring home many things to share with you – art projects; math, science and language activities; stories; games; and more. Your interest in and appreciation of these special projects is extremely important in encouraging and stimulating your child's desire to learn and grow.

In order to help with our projects, you can collect pine cones, newspapers and brown paper bags of all sizes. You also can suggest beautiful picture books and seasonal stories that are fitting for November reading. Anything you would like to contribute to enhance our November study and play would be appreciated. Happy November!

Sincerely,

NOVEMBER ALPHABET

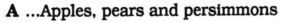

A ...Apples, pears and persimmons

B ...Bundles of hay stacked in barns

C ...Chestnuts roasting on the hearth

D ...Days of autumn splendor

E ...Embers glowing beneath warm fires

F ...Fine feathered friends

G ...Gorgeous autumn skies

H ...Happy Thanksgiving!

I ...Indians helped celebrate the first Thanksgiving

J ...Jars of jam made from autumn fruits

K ...Keeping traditions made long ago

L ...Leaves cover the ground

M ...Maize – the Indian word for corn

N ...Nuts stored in squirrels' nests

O ...Overhead, birds fly south

P ...Pumpkin pie and persimmon pudding

Q ...Quite a wonderful month!

R ...Reaping harvests

S ...Season of thanksgiving

T ...Turkey tails and turkey tales to tell

U ...Underground burrows prepared

V ...Verge of winter

W ...Windy days

X ...X-tra special season

Y ...Yellow fields

Z ...Zesty dishes for family feasts

NOVEMBER

Sunday	Monday	Tuesday	Wednesday	Thursday	Friday	Saturday

HOW TO USE THE NOVEMBER CALENDAR

Use the calendar to:

. . . find on what day of the week the first day of November falls.
. . . count the number of days in November.
. . . find the number on the calendar which represents November.
. . . mark the birthdays of "November babies" in your room.
. . . mark special days

- Sandwich Day (November 3)
- Veteran's Day (November 11)
- National Children's Book Week (November 13-19)
- Thanksgiving Day (Last Thursday in November)
- etc.

CALENDAR
ART

NOVEMBER CLASSROOM MANAGEMENT CHART

CLASSROOM HELPERS

COCK-A-DOODLE-DOO!

YOUR TEACHER IS PROUD OF YOU!

I am thankful for

_____

_____

TEACHER'S HELPER

NAME TAG

NOVEMBER

BOOKMARKS FOR
BOOK LOVERS

November... the perfect time to curl up with a good book!

BECAUSE WE LOVE
OUR LIBRARY

We do not speak above a whisper – of all of the treasures of the library, silence is golden.

We always return or renew books before they are overdue.

We treat books with care and respect.

We learn where things are in the library.

We visit the library often and discover many wonderful things!

We do not put books away unless we are sure where they belong.

We tell our teacher or librarian about lost or damaged books.

We tell our friends about books we have enjoyed.

We take pride in our library and learn from what it has to offer.

THE PLEDGE OF ALLEGIANCE

I pledge allegiance to the flag
of the United States of America,
and to the republic for which it stands,
one nation, under God, indivisible,
with liberty and justice for all.

TURKEYS AND OTHER FINE FEATHERED FRIENDS

Major Objective:
Children will learn the names, habits and distinguishing features of feathered fowl and simple facts related to the hatching of animals from eggs.

Things To Do:

- Read *Chickens Aren't the Only Ones* by Ruth Heller (see page 77) to the children. Then involve the children in the construction of the bulletin board on page 24.

- Reproduce the "Fine Feathered Friends" booklet cover (page 25) and the following seven pattern/activity pages (pages 26-32) in quantities to meet the needs of the class. Each day, present one pattern/activity page and have the children complete the activity and color the page. On the eighth day, help the children cut each page to make an egg shape. Help the children punch a hole in the top of each egg (including the booklet cover) and tie the pages together with yarn to make flip books.

- Give each child a copy of the story of *The Little Red Hen and the Grain of Wheat* (page 34). After reading the story to the children, ask the children to illustrate the story on several sheets of drawing paper. Help the children punch holes in their drawings and tie the pages together with yarn (placing the story page on top) to make booklets.

- Distribute copies of the finger puppets on page 35. Let the children work in small groups to act out the story of the Little Red Hen.

- Create a display of books, pictures, and other information about various kinds of fowl. Discuss a different bird each day.

- Let one week in November be "turkey week." Each day, present unusual and interesting facts about turkeys (see *Wonders of Turkeys*, page 78) and read books about turkeys (see pages 77 & 78). Decorate the room with pictures of turkeys and construct the bulletin board on page 38. Involve the children in turkey projects (see pages 39-44), and have a "turkey gobbling" contest!

Construction:

1. Reproduce the turkey, hen, quail, pheasant, peacock and duck patterns (pages 26-31) to make cutting patterns for the children.
2. Have the children cut out the fowl and color them with crayons or markers.
3. Cut the caption "Fine Feathered Friends" out of construction paper.
4. Arrange the children's patterns on the board to make an attractive display.

Variation:

• Have the children draw, color and cut out their own "fowl" friends!

FINE FEATHERED FRIENDS

By _____

Date _____

STRUT
MR. TURKEY

Strut Mr. Turkey,
Big and fat,
Strut Mr. Turkey,
Just like that,
Strut Mr. Turkey,
Strut, strut, strut.

Strut Mr. Turkey,
Prance and play,
Thanksgiving Day
Is on the way,
So strut today,
Strut, strut, strut.

MY
BLACK HEN

Hickety, pickety, my black hen,
She lays eggs for gentlemen;
Gentlemen come every day
To see what my black hen doth lay.

QUAIL IN HIDING

Find and circle 6 quail in the picture.
Color the picture.

PLEASANT PHEASANT

Have you seen a pleasant pheasant?
Where could the pleasant pheasant be?
Color all the spaces marked with a "P"
and a pleasant pheasant you will see.

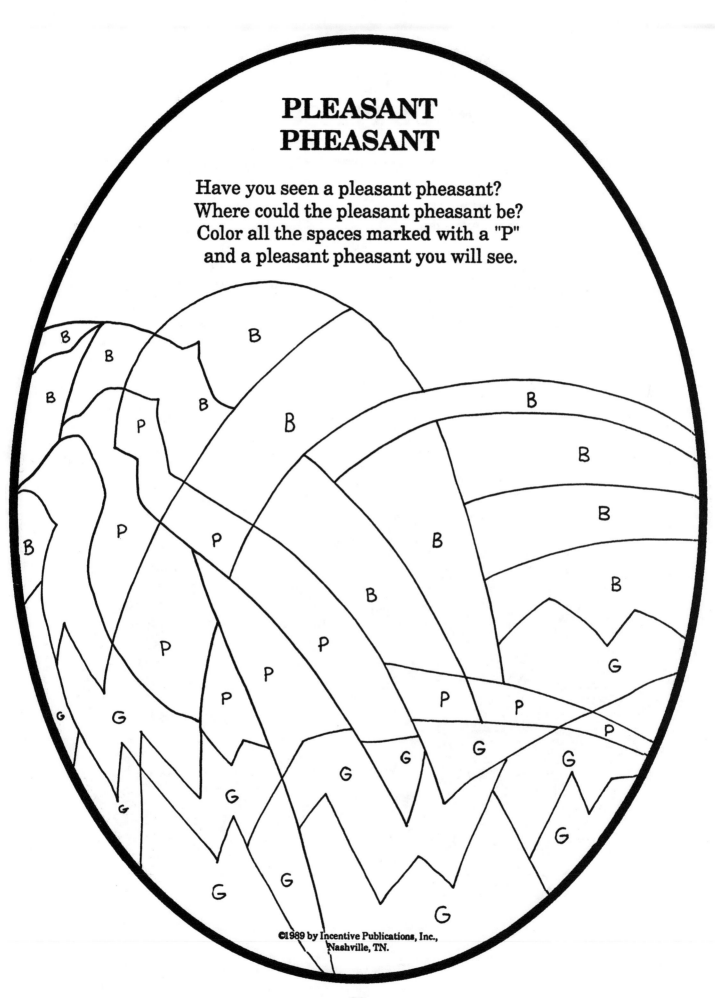

FIVE
PROUD PEACOCKS

Five proud peacocks
Preening and prancing,
One pranced away
Then there were four.

Four proud peacocks
Preening and prancing,
One pranced away
Then there were three.

Three proud peacocks
Preening and prancing,
One flew away
Then there were two.

Two proud peacocks
Preening and prancing,
One flew away
Then there was one.

One proud peacock
Left alone,
Too proud to prance.

LOOK-ALIKE DUCKS

Three ducks look alike, but only two are twins.
Circle the twin ducks.

OLD MOTHER GOOSE

Old Mother Goose, when
 She wanted to wander,
Would ride through the air
 On a very fine gander.

Mother Goose had a house,
 'Twas built in a wood,
An owl at the door
 For a porter stood.

She had a son Jack,
 A plain-looking lad,
He was not very good,
 Nor yet very bad.

She sent him to market,
 A live goose he bought:
"Here! mother," says he,
 "It will not go for nought."

Jack's goose and her gander
 Grew very fond;
They'd both eat together,
 Or swim in one pond.

Jack found one fine morning,
 As I have been told,
His goose had laid him
 An egg of pure gold.

Jack rode to his mother,
 The news for to tell.
She called him a good boy,
 And said it was well.

And Old Mother Goose
 The goose saddled soon,
And mounting its back,
 Flew up to the moon.

MATCH THE BARNYARD MOTHERS AND BABIES

Draw a line to connect each barnyard baby to its mother.
One has been done for you.

THE LITTLE RED HEN AND THE GRAIN OF WHEAT

One day the Little Red Hen was scratching in the farmyard
when she found a grain of wheat.
"Who will plant the wheat?" she asked.

"Not I," said the duck.
 "Not I," said the cat.
  "Not I," said the dog.
"Very well then," said the Little Red Hen, "I will."
So, she planted the grain of wheat.

After some time, the wheat grew tall and ripe.
 "Who will cut the wheat?" asked the Little Red Hen.
"Not I," said the duck.
 "Not I," said the cat.
  "Not I," said the dog.
"Very well then, I will," said the Little Red Hen.
 So, she cut the wheat.

"Now," she said, "who will thresh the wheat?"
 "Not I," said the duck.
  "Not I," said the cat.
   "Not I," said the dog.
"Very well then, I will," said the Little Red Hen.
 So, she threshed the wheat.

When the wheat was threshed, she said, "Who will
 take the wheat to the mill to have it ground into flour?"
"Not I," said the duck.
 "Not I," said the cat.
  "Not I," said the dog.
"Very well then, I will," said the Little Red Hen.
 So, she took the wheat to the mill.

When the wheat was ground into flour, she said, "Who
 will make this flour into bread?"
"Not I," said the duck.
 "Not I," said the cat.
  "Not I," said the dog.
"Very well then, I will," said the Little Red Hen.
 And she baked a lovely loaf of bread.

Then she said, "Who will eat the bread?"
 "Oh, I will!" said the duck.
  "Oh, I will!" said the cat.
   "Oh, I will!" said the dog.
"Oh, no you won't," said the Little Red Hen, "I will!"
 And she called her chicks and shared the bread with them.

LITTLE RED HEN
FINGER PUPPETS

Color and cut out the finger puppets.
Tape the puppets together and act out the story.

BREAD AND BUTTER RECIPES

Little Red Hen's Easy-To-Make-Bread

Ingredients:
1/2 yeast cake
1 cup warm water
1/2 tablespoon sugar

1/2 teaspoon salt
2 cups flour
1/2 stick butter

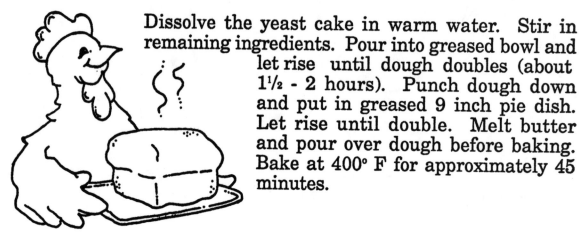

Dissolve the yeast cake in warm water. Stir in remaining ingredients. Pour into greased bowl and let rise until dough doubles (about 1½ - 2 hours). Punch dough down and put in greased 9 inch pie dish. Let rise until double. Melt butter and pour over dough before baking. Bake at 400° F for approximately 45 minutes.

Better Butter

Ingredients:
1 pint whipping cream
salt

Equally divide the whipping cream into two 2½ pint jars (with screw-on lids).

Shake the jars as hard as you can until butter forms.

Use a spoon to dip the butter into a bowl.

Stir in a dash of salt.

Spread on hot bread.

(Extra good with a little honey!)

ROOSTER SHOW-OFF

To "show off" good work, help the children color and cut out rooster show-offs to attach to their papers. Show-offs make attractive bulletin board displays and great "take homes"!

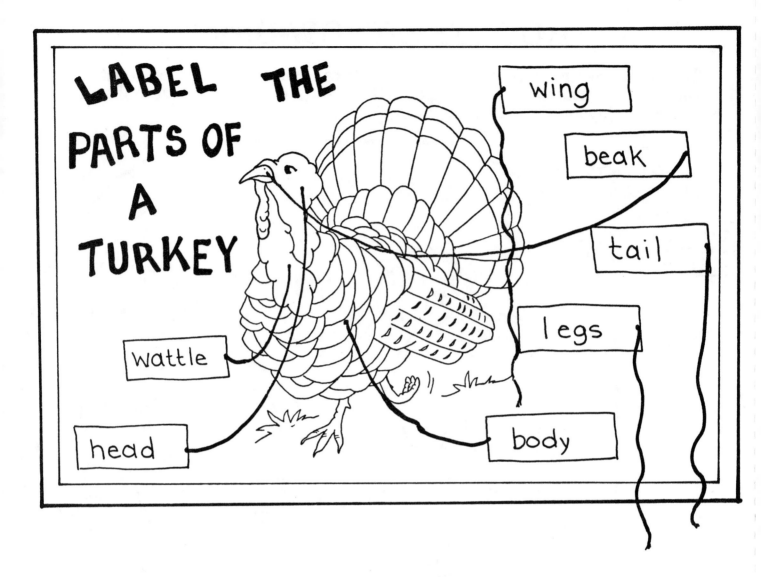

Construction:

1. Reproduce the turkey pattern on page 26 and color it with markers or cut it out of construction paper.
2. Cut the caption "Label The Parts Of A Turkey" out of construction paper.
3. Write each of the following turkey "parts" on a strip of cardboard: head, wing, beak, wattle, legs, body, tail.
4. Assemble the board.
5. Instruct the children to pin the labels on the correct turkey "parts" for a manipulative bulletin board activity. Assist as necessary.

Variation:

- Label the turkey by connecting the cardboard strips to the correct "parts" with strips of yarn or string (shown above).

STAND-ALONE TURKEY

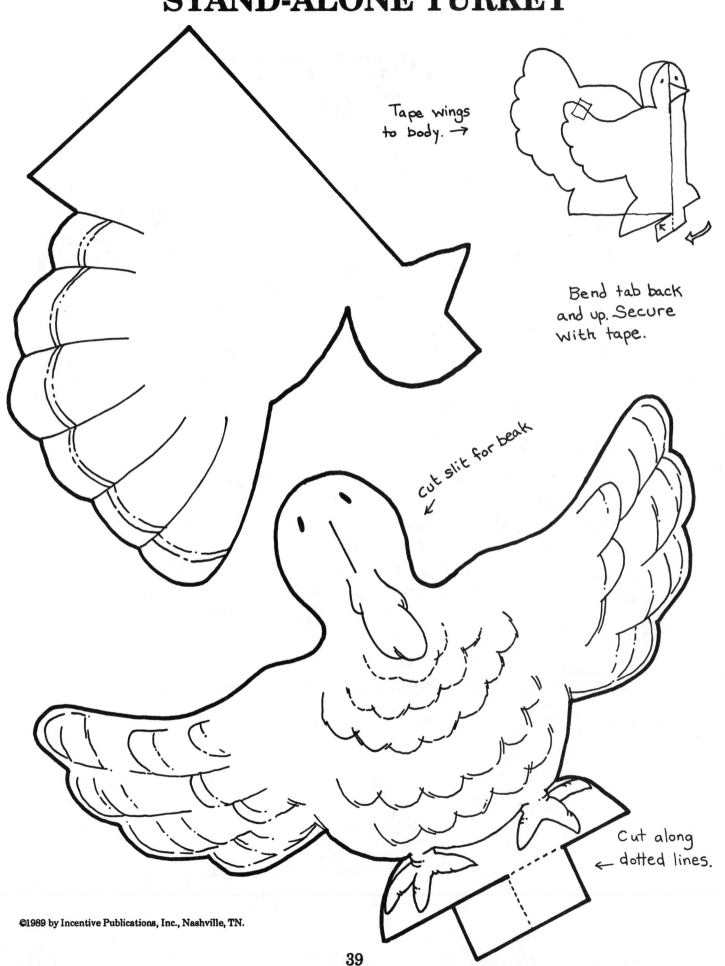

Tape wings to body. →

Bend tab back and up. Secure with tape.

cut slit for beak

Cut along dotted lines.

PARTICIPATION TURKEY

Children will enjoy participating in the construction of this 3-D turkey!

What To Use:
1 large and 1 medium size brown
    paper bag
newspaper
rubber bands or string
construction paper
paste
tape
sticks (approx. 15" each)

What To Do:

1. Stuff a large and a medium size brown paper bag with newspaper.
2. Tightly gather the opening of the smaller bag and secure it with rubber bands or string.
3. Place the secured end of the smaller bag in the opening of the larger bag. Tightly gather the opening and secure it with rubber bands or string. (Be sure the secured end of the smaller bag is inside the larger bag.)

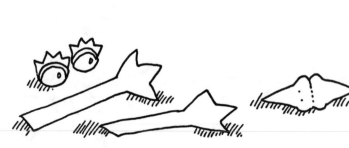

MEGAN is thankful for her Mom.

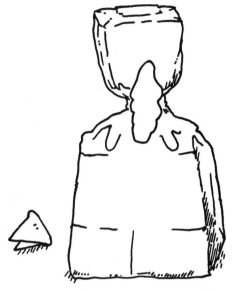

4. Use the patterns on pages 42 and 43 to cut eyes, a beak and a wattle out of construction paper. Paste or tape the features to the paper bag.

5. Have the children gather sticks (each approximately 15 inches long). Each child may cut a feather out of construction paper (pattern on page 42) and write his or her name and a Thanksgiving message on the feather. Have the children use masking or cellophane tape to attach their feathers to the sticks.

6. Punch enough holes in the bag to hold all of the children's feathers. Let each child place his or her feather in a hole to complete the 3-D turkey.

Hint: You may want the children to place their feathers in this kind of pattern. The wing feathers point down (laying side by side) and the tail feathers point straight up.

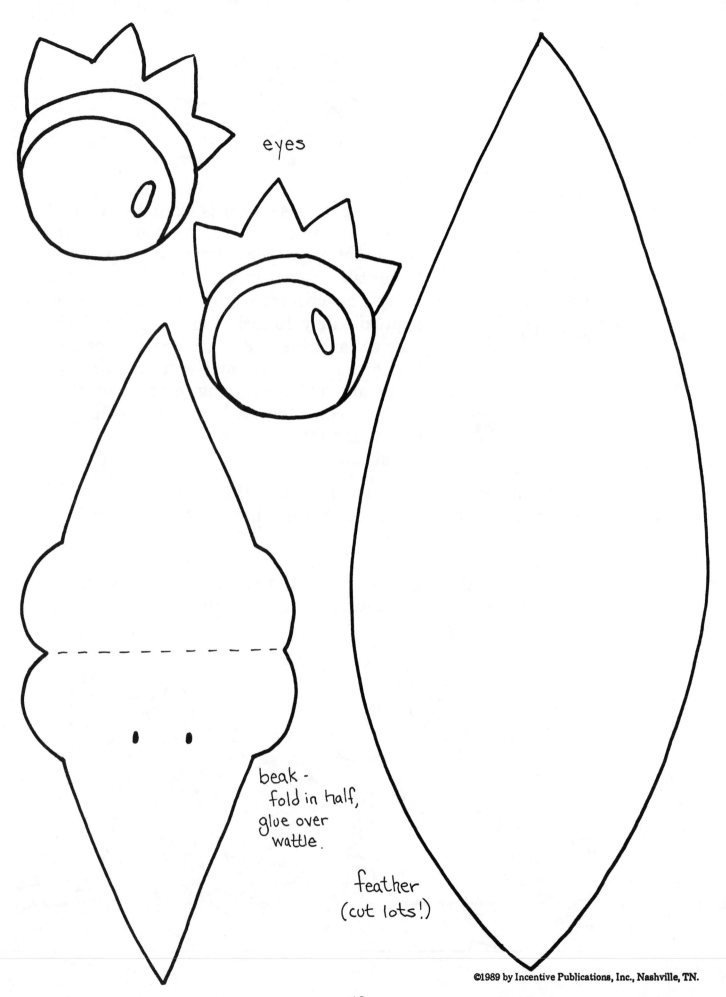

eyes

beak -
fold in half,
glue over
wattle.

feather
(cut lots!)

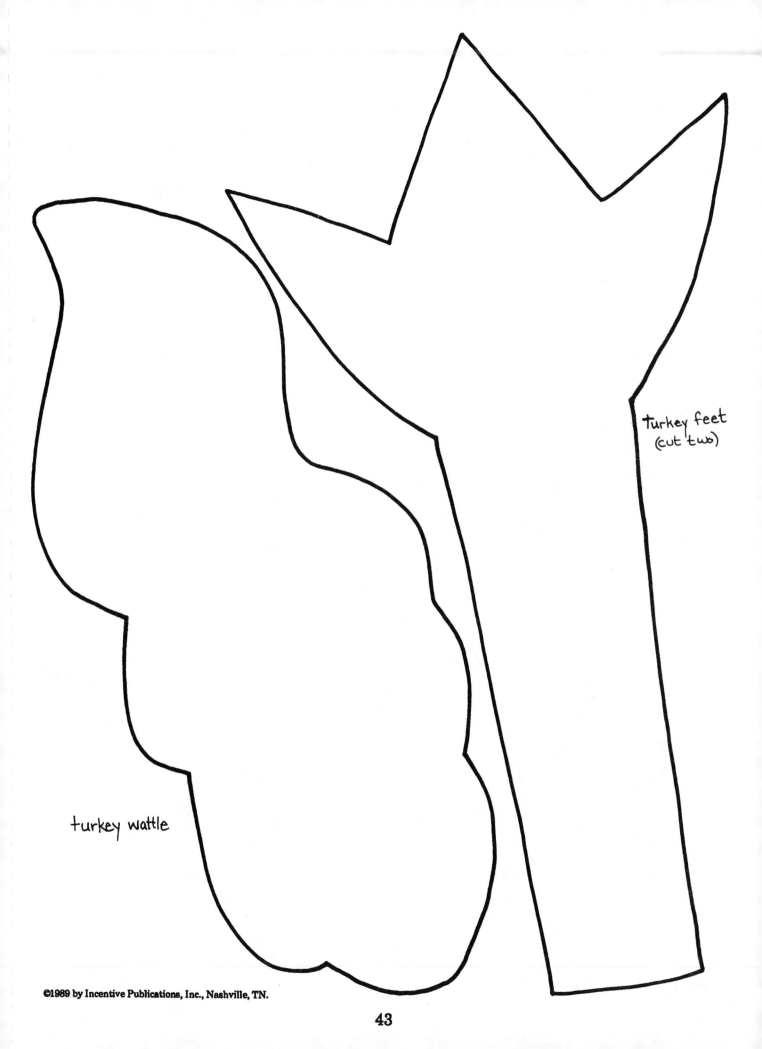

turkey feet
(cut two)

turkey wattle

THREE TERRIFIC TURKEYS

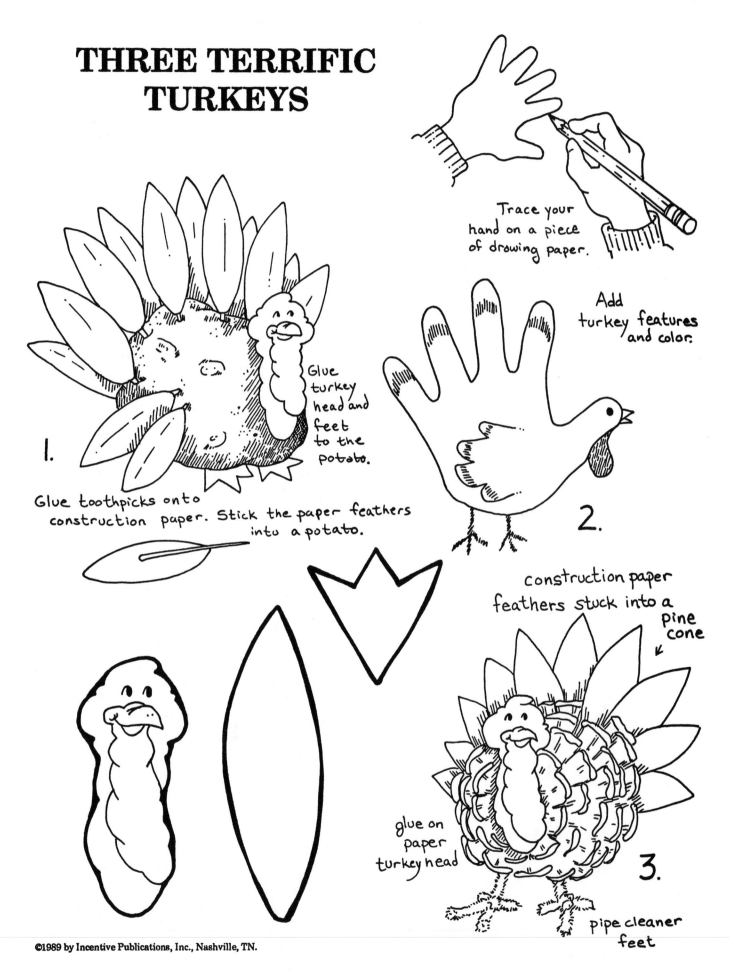

Trace your hand on a piece of drawing paper.

Add turkey features and color.

1.

Glue turkey head and feet to the potato.

Glue toothpicks onto construction paper. Stick the paper feathers into a potato.

2.

construction paper feathers stuck into a pine cone

glue on paper turkey head

3.

pipe cleaner feet

THANKSGIVING
A TIME TO BE THANKFUL

Major Objective:
Children will express their thankfulness for things in their everyday world and will explore feelings and relationships as they learn about the first Thanksgiving. Children also will learn about balanced meals and the habits of animals preparing for winter.

Things To Do:

- Reproduce the "Time To Be Thankful" banner (page 50) for each child. Have the children decorate their banners with crayons or markers. Punch holes in the banners and run yarn through the holes to make necklaces. The children will enjoy wearing their banners during the school day and on their way home, too!

- Let half of the class be Pilgrims and the other half be Indians for a day. Help the children make costumes (see pages 68-71). At lunch time, have the children "pair off" so that each Pilgrim child is sitting with an Indian child. Ask the children to discuss how they think the Pilgrims and Indians became friends.

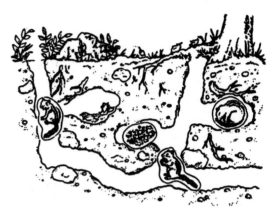

- Gather books and materials containing information about animals that gather food and make "nests" in preparation for winter. Display the materials and present new information each day for a week. At the end of the week, help the children complete the activity "It's Harvest Time For The Animals, Too!" (page 59).

- Provide the children with white paper plates, scissors, paste, and old magazines. Have groups of children look through the magazines to find pictures of foods that would make a balanced meal. Have the children in each group cut out the pictures and paste them on a paper plate to show a balanced meal.

- Reproduce the certificate on page 75 in quantities to meet the needs of the class. Complete a certificate for each child and present the certificates on the last day before Thanksgiving vacation.

Construction:

1. Enlarge the turkey pattern on page 47 and color it with markers or cut it out of construction paper.

2. Have each child cut a turkey feather out of construction paper (pattern on page 48) and write or draw on the feather one thing for which he or she is thankful. Help the children paste their feathers on the turkey.

3. Cut the caption "Time To Be Thankful!" out of construction paper.

4. Assemble the board as shown.

Variation:

- Cover the classroom door with butcher paper and attach the turkey (with the children's feathers) and the banner on page 50 to the door.

Suggested Reading:
One Tough Turkey (see page 78).

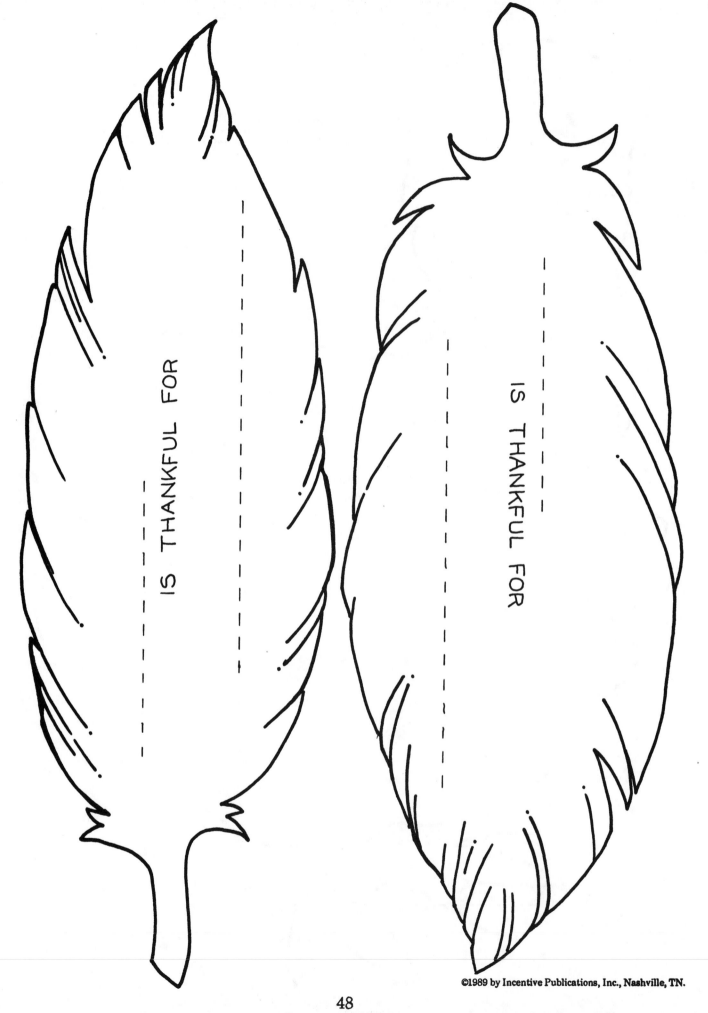

IS THANKFUL FOR

IS THANKFUL FOR

THANKSGIVING
DOORKNOB DECORATION

Color and cut out this doorknob decoration.
Hang it on your door in celebration of Thanksgiving

HAVE A

HAPPY

THANKSGIVING

NOVEMBER, A TIME TO BE THANKFUL!

Name _____

A THANKSGIVING PICTOGRAPH

Draw pictures to show things for which
you are thankful.

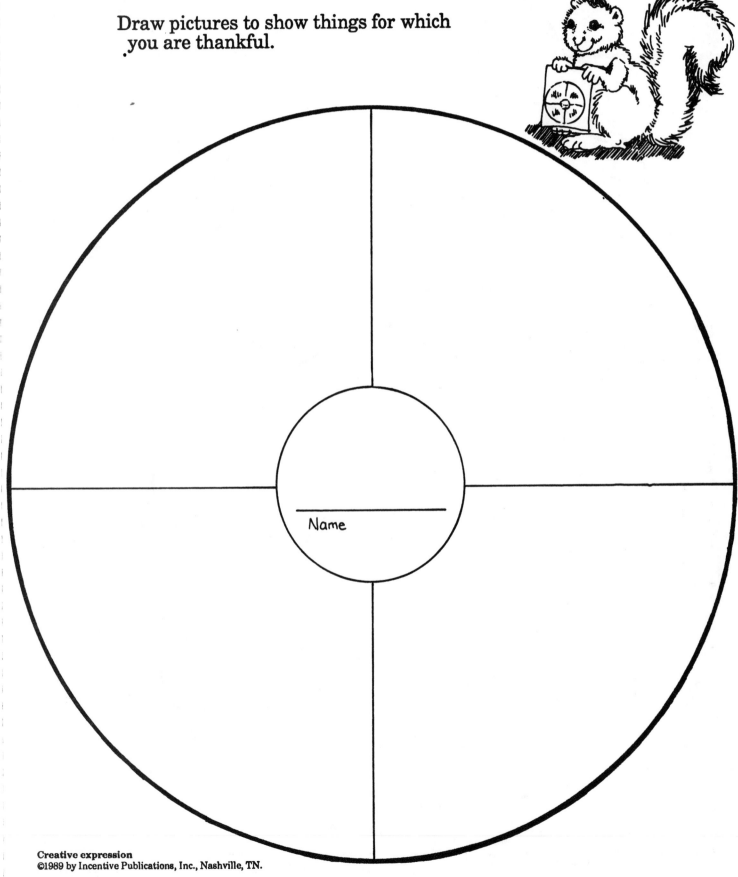

Name

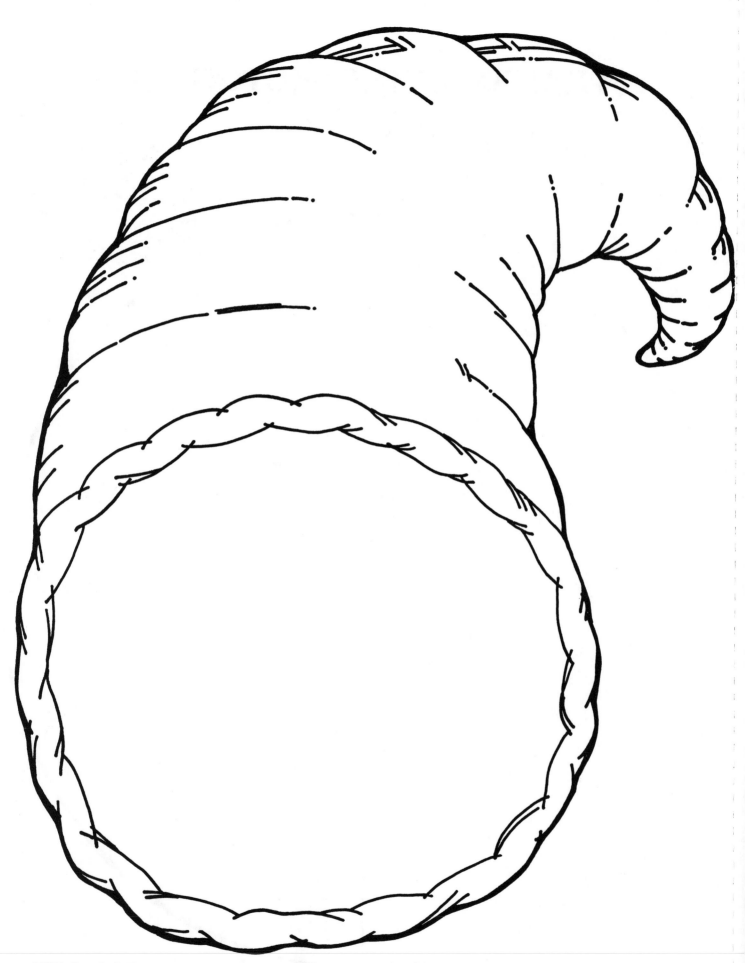

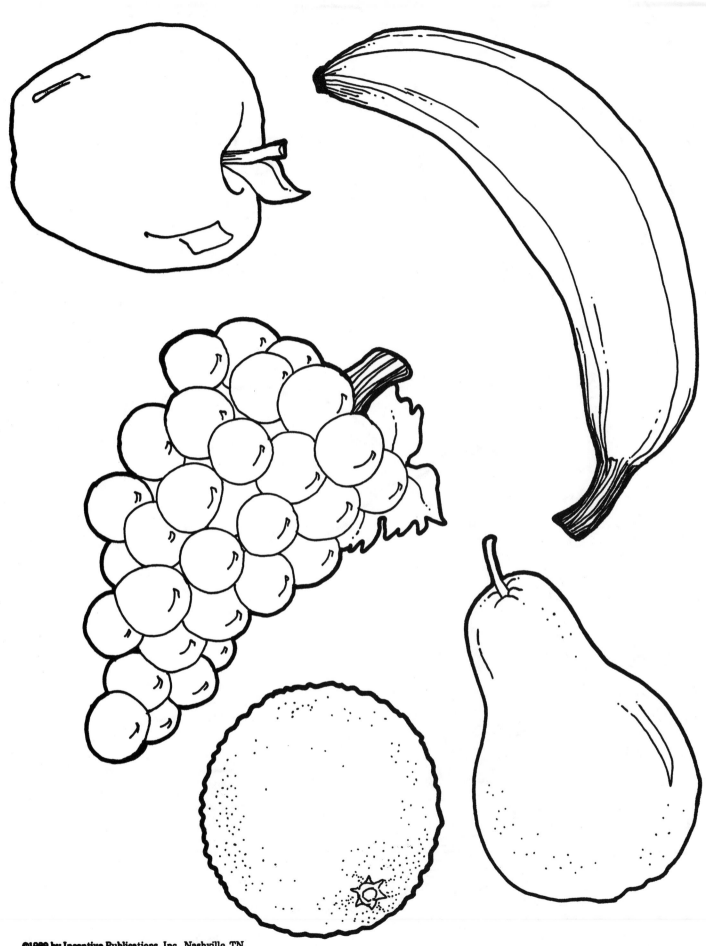

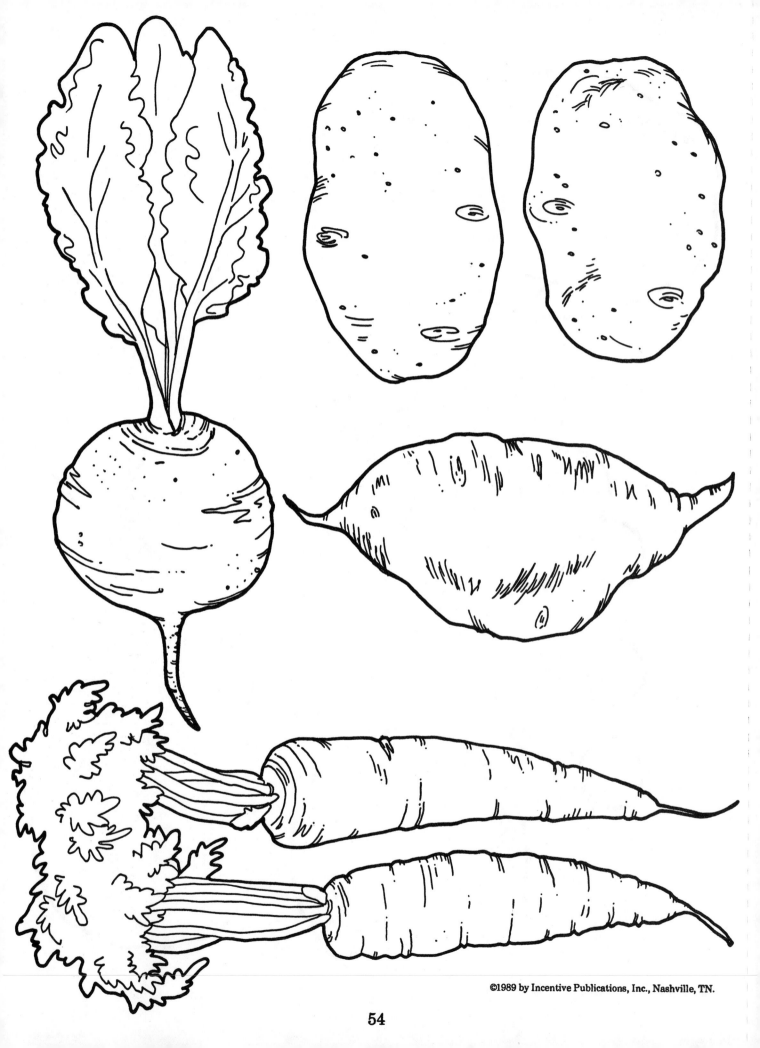

Construction:

1. Reproduce the barn pattern on page 57 and color it with markers or cut it out of construction paper.

2. Help the children make hand-print turkeys (directions on page 44). Have each child write "Love" and his or her name on a turkey.

3. Cut the caption "Hands Up For Thanksgiving!" out of construction paper.

4. Assemble the board as shown above.

5. On the last day before the Thanksgiving holidays, let the children take their turkeys home for Thanksgiving cards.

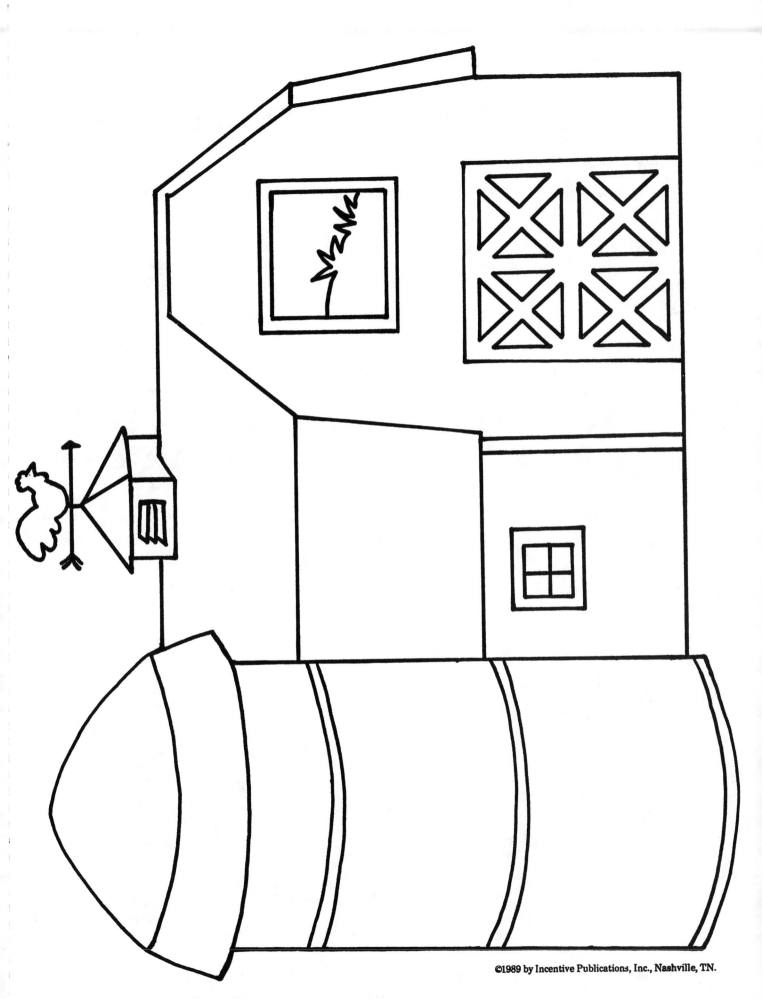

THANKSGIVING DAY SURPRISE

Connect the dots from 1 to 12 to find a Thanksgiving Day surprise.

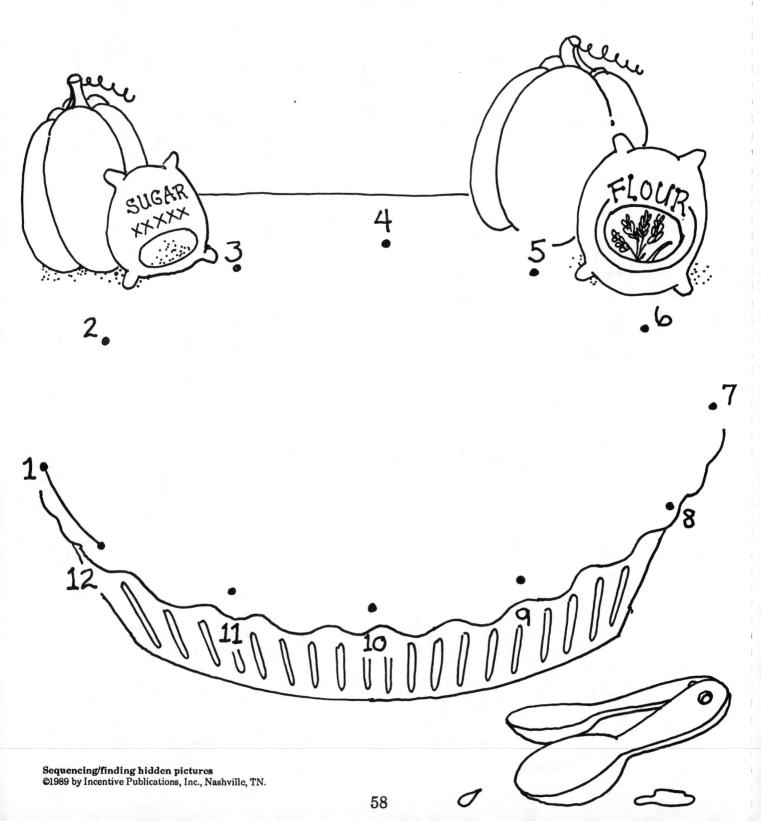

IT'S HARVEST TIME
FOR THE ANIMALS, TOO!

Reproduce the patterns below and on pages 60-62 in quantities sufficient to meet the needs of the class. Have the children color the patterns, cut them out, and paste the animals and nuts in the correct "homes."

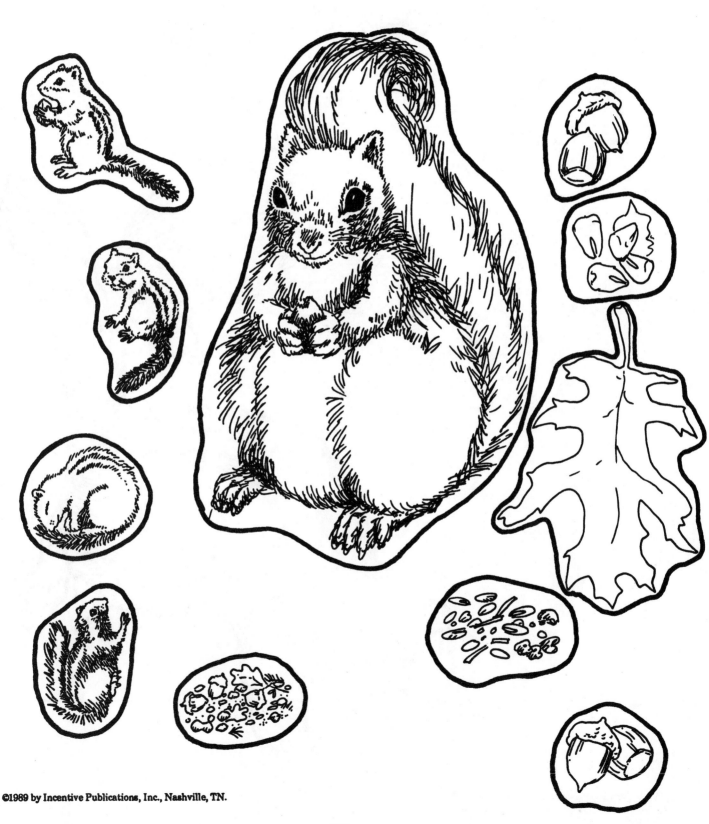

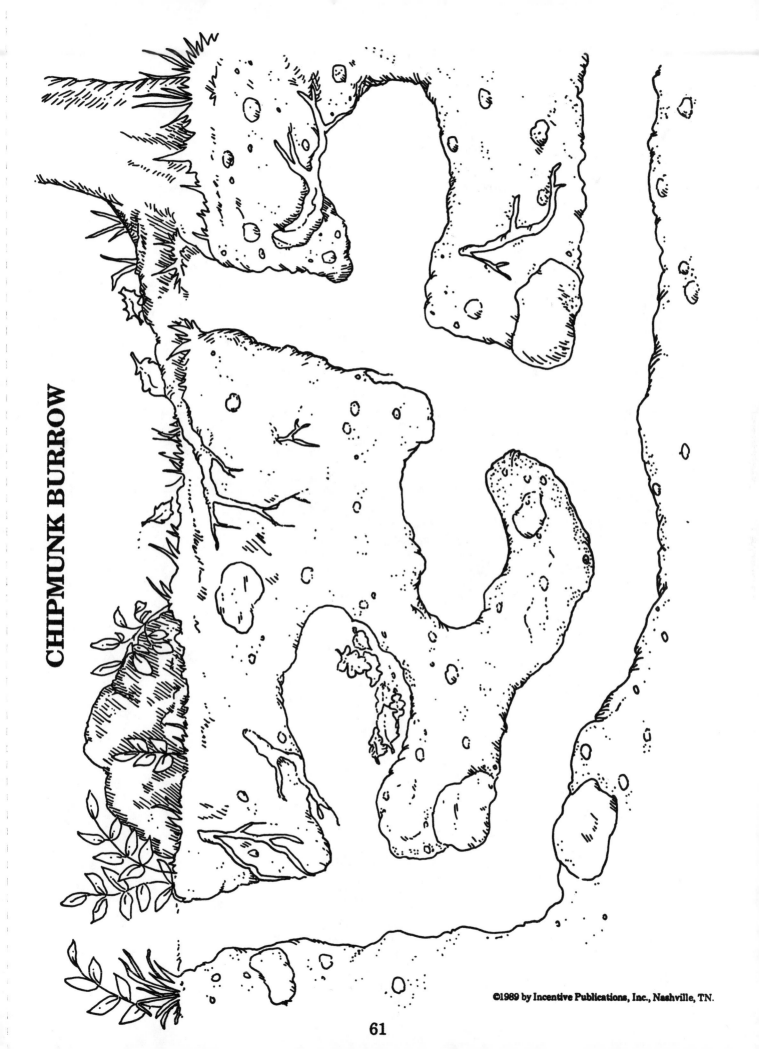

CHIPMUNK BURROW

SQUIRREL NEST

HOW MANY ACORNS?

This little squirrel is getting ready for winter.
How many acorns do you see? _____

Counting
©1989 by Incentive Publications, Inc., Nashville, TN.

PAPER BAG INDIAN VEST

Cut a large grocery bag
as indicated by the
dotted lines.

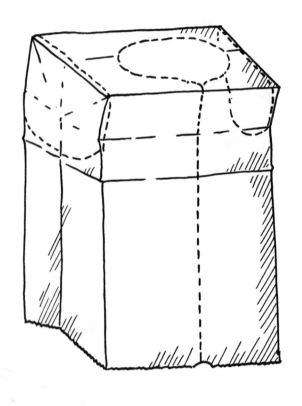

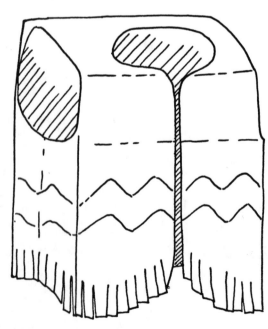

Decorate
and cut a
fringe with scissors.

INDIAN HEADDRESS

Decorate the
headband.
Tape it together
and add one or
more feathers.

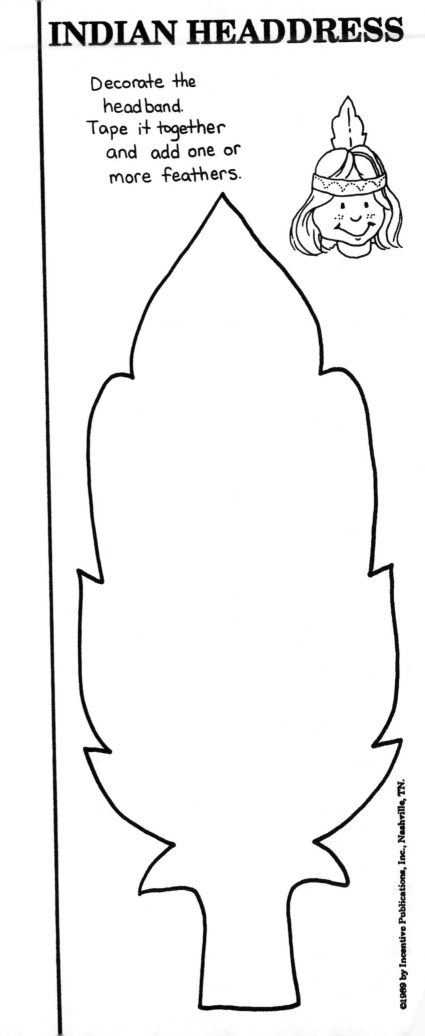

PILGRIM HAT

Use this for a shoe buckle, also.

FOLD

FOLD

fold

PILGRIM COLLAR

Fold a piece of 12" x 18" construction paper in half. Trace the collar pattern & cut out.

THE FOUR BASIC FOOD GROUPS

BREADS AND CEREALS

OATS

MEAT POULTRY AND FISH

EGGS

SAUS

TUNA

EAT FOODS FROM EACH GROUP EVERY DAY!

FRUITS AND VEGETABLES

CORN

PEAS

MILK AND DAIRY PRODUCTS

COTTAGE CHEESE

BUTTER

MILK

YOUGU

A HEALTHY FEAST

Cut and paste five foods on the table to show a healthy Thanksgiving dinner.

Name _____

THE FIRST THANKSGIVING FEAST

Color the foods that you think might have been
served at the first Thanksgiving feast.
Was it a balanced meal?

Decision making
©1989 by Incentive Publications, Inc., Nashville, TN.

Dear _____,

Your teacher is thankful
for you because _____

_____

_____

_____

Teacher _____

Date _____

NOVEMBER BULLETIN
BOARD BORDERS

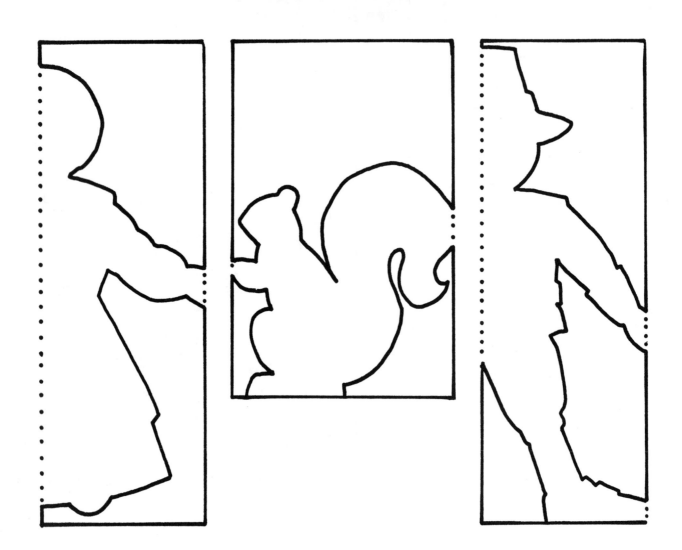

Accordion fold paper strips to match the size of the pattern.
Tape or trace pattern onto paper and cut.
Be sure dotted lines touch edges.

BIBLIOGRAPHY

Animals Born Alive and Well. Ruth Heller. Putnam Publishing Group.
The beautifully illustrated pages in this book present mammals and their characteristics in a manner that will capture and hold the interest of children. This picture book is the perfect companion to *Chickens Aren't The Only Ones*, also by Ruth Heller.

Arthur's Thanksgiving. Marc Brown. Little, Brown & Co.
Arthur is elected to direct the Thanksgiving play, but no one will volunteer to be the turkey. The hilarious solution will delight children.

Chickens Aren't the Only Ones. Ruth Heller. Grosset & Dunlap.
This delightful picture book is full of surprises concerning animals that are hatched from eggs.

Cranberry Thanksgiving. Wende & Harry Devlin. Parents' Magazine Press.
Maggie and her grandmother invite two very special guests for Thanksgiving dinner. Grandmother dislikes Mr. Whiskers until he saves her secret cranberry bread recipe.

The First Snowfall. Anne and Harlow Rockwell. Macmillan.
This short, simple story with its bold, full-color illustrations captures the special magic of a child's day in a snow-covered world.

Goodnight, Goodnight. Eve Rice. Greenwillow Books.
"Goodnight" creeps all over town through the strikingly illustrated pages of this easy-to-read book.

Goodnight Moon. Margaret Wise Brown. Harper & Row.
A little bunny says goodnight to all of the familiar things around him. The gentle, lulling text and the beautiful four-color illustrations make this a perfect book for the end of the day.

Indian Two Feet and His Eagle Feather. Margaret Friskey. Children's Press.
A little Indian boy earns an eagle feather and learns a great lesson about wisdom and bravery when he saves his village from a flood.

It's Thanksgiving. Jack Prelutsky. Greenwillow Books.
This delightful book contains lighthearted poetry covering every aspect of Thanksgiving.

Little Chief. Syd Hoff. Harper & Row.
When a wagon train comes to Little Chief's valley, he saves the children from a stampede of buffaloes and gains the friends he has been wanting so desperately.

Mousekin's Woodland Sleepers. Edna Miller. Prentice-Hall.
In a gust of wind, Mousekin loses his home and must set out to find a woodland creature who will share its home with him.

One Terrific Thanksgiving. Marjorie Weinman Sharmat. Holiday House.
Irving Morris Bear asks his friends to hide his food so that it will be safe for Thanksgiving Day. When he changes his mind and wants the food returned, chaos takes over and teaches him a lesson.

One Tough Turkey. Steven Kroll. Holiday House.
In this humorous story, the turkeys do hilarious things to the Pilgrims when the Pilgrims try to capture them for Thanksgiving Day dinner.

Sometimes It's Turkey, Sometimes It's Feathers. Lorna Balian. Abingdon.
Mrs. Gumm finds an egg that hatches into a spectacular turkey that she grows to love.

Thanksgiving At the Tappleton's. Eileen Spinelli. Harper & Row Jr. Books.
When the turkey gets away before the Thanksgiving dinner occurs, the Tappleton family has a wonderful holiday anyway.

Thanksgiving Day. Gail Gibbons. Holiday House.
This historic "time line" of the first Thanksgiving's origins and traditions is presented in a colorful manner which allows the reader to compare the past and present.

The Turkey Girl. Betty Baker. Macmillan.
Tally the turkey girl, who spends her days and nights taking care of the town's turkeys, learns one cold winter that bravery and a little turkey magic can make dreams come true.

Wonders Of Turkeys. Sigmund A. Lavine and Vincent Scuro. Dodd, Mead & Co.
This book contains everything you ever wanted to know about turkeys — facts, folklore and more.

INDEX